Moon-

Forrest Mifflin

Copyright © 2012 Forrest Mifflin

All rights reserved.

ISBN: 1468162195
ISBN-13: 978-1468162196

Front Cover: Photo courtesy Liz Nilsson

DEDICATION

This work is dedicated to all those that have brought love into my life. Without which, not a single word could have been written, and with which, every word ever written is not enough to say; thank you.

Contents

At last..8
Moonwalk..8
It's Beautiful 9
Sun Down 9
Mass Appeal 10
First Light 10
Moon Found 11
Moon Phases...11
Eclipsed 12
What I would Give 12
Your Name 13
jiminy...14
Just an Opening 14
From Them, to Me, for You 15
Marking 17
The Hand 17
Stardust Covered Lens....................................18
Your Attraction...19
Just a Crush?..20
Love's Journey 20

Kissed Once	21
In a Moment's Breath	22
Changed Scenery	23
What I Want	24
Being There	24
Rant, Ramble, Worship	25
Lakeside	28
Harboring	29
Fish	29
By Love	30
Love's Division	31
Blue Knight	31
You Know	33
Mark Your Calendar	33
You Again	34
Ready	35
Her Dawn, My Birdsong	35
Right now?	36
Climatic	37
Rapturously	38
Being with You	39
Close Calls	39
Glazed	40

Questioning Love	40
my Capture	41
Timing My Breaths	42
On the Curb	43
Homecoming Day	43
Stillness	44
Saying Goodbye	44
Surviving	44
Preoccupied	45
The Forest	46
a la natural	48
Your Choice	49
A Jug	49
Soothing	50
Rewind	50
This One Time	51
Partial Delivery	51
Two into One	53
Flights of	53
Redemption	54
Consigned	55
Absent thee	56
Take Heart	56

INTRODUCTION

I'm stuck. Just sitting here trying to figure out how to introduce my book, I decide to browse Facebook for some inspiration. I have lots of friends that write lots of things and many of the poems in this book were first shared there. Since many of these poems were taken from instant message chats, it seems only fitting that the best introduction for this work would come from a chat session I just had with my significant other. I ask her, "What would you say about my poetry?" She replies, "Poetry that can be enjoyed many times over. Each time I read it I can interpret another meaning. There are layers of mystique to your poems."

Right, that is the message I want to convey; these are not only poems about the love between two lovers, but also a reflection on the love and connection to the divine. The fundamental human need to search and find these two intertwining threads is the basic ingredient to purpose and meaning. To me *this* is what life is all about. When someone says life is short, or time is short, I hear something that says, "Move to love today; find, express and embrace that which makes life whole, joyous and complete. Be in Love. It is what we do, what we say and what we feel; the fullest extent of being alive."

I can write about it, but you and I are living it.

Right?

The memory tides of You will spring forever from within heart's flow of love.

At last...

Against the purple-violet night sky,
filled with millions of twinkling eyes-
One prismatic moon lit snowflake,
illuminated all eternity-
You smiled...

Moonwalk

Whisper nothing to the Moon,
For tonight the Moon is Full,
free of secrets
Strongly pulling away any
fear of closeness
To reflect Love's Light
in being together
Brightening the nightscape,
shadowing Our walk
The Friend keeps an Eye
in the Sky, on Us
Only Love is the course,
the measure and the destination.

It's Beautiful

With silvery strands, the luminous flux enters
the golden inner sanctums of my Being
Hewing the surface, a diamond's brilliance
making the heart truly fitting
To return the jewel of my contentment;
the image of Your face...

Sun Down

Gaze into the setting Sun
and watch the sky blush the
arrival of Our Moon
Night, Time of Lover's peak
with new fragrances arriving
in the Garden valley
The air can now cool a body's
heat, letting the earth sigh
with pleasant relief
Rest now, ancient of ancients
while Your dear ones sleep
dreaming of Your return

Mass Appeal

Looking upon you again, old friend,
are you a talisman or a temptress-
or maybe both while lounging there?
You're beaming again, too!
As a face you smile to the sky, and
as the eye of the night, you wink.
Such a flirt you are, when so full!
It is so wonderful to see you so open,
as usually you have shy, hidden parts.
Naturally, that just makes you all the
more alluring, mysterious and seductive.
And just like the Love that you inspire,
no one can ignore you in any phase!

First Light

Daring one, my true companion
What would I be, without a moon?
A dead world, with no breath for song
A Beautiful rock, collages of creativity
Connected to vastness, an empty silence
Craters of history, without any lessons
A pointless circling, waiting for the end
Daring one, my true companion
What would I be, without a sun?
The Dawn...

Moon Found

I scanned the sky
this daring night
clouds, shuffling by
causing a small fright.
There! just to the South.
The Moon being fresh
with the faint Star
just to the right.

Moon Phases

There are never more lovers than dreamers
Forever changing places as conspirators
Luminous, shadowed, fading in dawn's glow
Opaque features, reflecting a faceless Sun
Caressing the last moment of Consciousness
Escaping with delight, all ecstatic awakenings
Speckled eastern horizon, sky pearl rising
Travel to Love's only setting; an open heart.

Eclipsed

'Twas a twinkling in the night sky,
A light movement which caught my eye.
It sends light in all directions and shape,
Looking away, my attention does not escape.
Captivating, subdued with power that's hidden,
My tongue is tied, my heart is smitten.
I want to breathe in that warm glow,
Please come to me, let me experience you.

What I would Give

From Her,
I would trade all treasures,
both future and past
for a single eyelash.
All those eyes reflect,
are Beauty and Love
In ONE Being

Your Name

Lovely is the name the Sunset brings
Creating infinite colors, the birds sing
Night comes to continue the call
Moon rises, the lovers' grand ball

Listen, as the summer breeze speaks
Resistance like a branch falls weak
Like a heart receiving full grace
Self-overcome leaving no trace

The clouds meander to cover stars
Eyes of heaven, sending joy in jars
Fires rage scorching the ground
Breath halts, waiting for the sound

Whispering echoes throughout existence
The word beautiful pales description
Powerful, radiant, completely surreal
A moving experience all can feel

How is it that all this came?
It's from saying your name.

jiminy

As if some angelic minstrels lay
between my ears and heart-
While saying Your name, is joyous
Hearing Your name feels beautiful-
Setting then, My Soul, as a longing
Cricket chirping in a Summer Night.

Just an Opening

When I first saw You, in the doorway You stood
the door was open, outside it's midday.
Here on the inside it's edgy and shadowed,
although, with You either space is hallowed.
I want to stay in and explore, scout...
You? You just want me to come out.

I have a present if You stay and play.
Up to You, it's Your Allowance anyway.

We dance...

Out the door, I follow You close
Your form melts my heart, I'm roasted.
I become a Green Dragon, I hiss secrets
of alchemy, majic, magnus and tantrics.
You giggle at me, and then smile,
this creates more inside cooking!

I become an Eagle, fly up a mile
the Dragon is fired, for not working.

From above I watch as You enter fields
Gathering others, planting seeds again.
I command the wind, it bends and yields
Purposely scattering seeds from Your hand.
They drop to the ground, spouting WEEEEEE!
The Eagle wants You... What will it BE?
All Love needs from You is an Opening.

From Them, to Me, for You

lovers meet at the stone alter to worship under the moon
bodies reflecting its dull light...brightening skin
the closeness makes ions become charged and
exit and enter between them
they can feel the exchange of intent
fears are bent away
now anticipated touches
caressed lightning streaks in their eyes
his will grounds her, she surrounds him
from every space they want to know and enter
each other, again and again
like they have never known this before
each time is more than the first and
the memory of the last....passes to
find remaining unknowns
they throw care and concern for anything

but their own pleasure.. off the cliff
and throw the limits to passion off of it
too
how mighty that IS
willful acts of passion and pleasure
nothing to be held back from lovers
so let me take it from them to you
because my Beloved
if you imagine it...it comes for you
arrives in your Life...faster than any
spell, wishing well or lucky charm
looking from inside me to inside you
if we touched or kissed before
then we will remember for sure
of our promise to return
here to surrender again at the alter
the universe cradled our need
to be together, we slept rocking
feeling the fall of love's slope
sliding...point of fear falling down
to some unknown...when really
this is no lark...but the lune
...for we rest peacefully, hammocked
in Our Crescent moon

Your Attraction

There is nothing outside of You the universe wants,
like plasma through space, carrying new beginnings
streaming supercharged excitement in pure vacuum,
a feeling of any heart touching the Friend's existence.
All joy, peace, contentment and happiness bubbles
forth, a new world, from the internal galactic center,
a gravity of truth that even light can only escape as
Love, to be born into every seeker's awareness.

Just a Crush?

Within the gathered Circle, You passed by the Outside
It wasn't Your Face, Smile or Your sideways Glance
that caught my Breath, slayed all Intent, stunned Mind.
Just Your Shadow landing upon Me, caused My
Impotence.

What's this about?
Putting my Cart before Your Horses.
Am I enthralled?
Sign me up for all Your Courses!
I will devour every book in Your library, even mysteries.
Recognize every possibility....join in all Your Histories.
You bring; Constant Expansion, No Conditions, No
Boundaries.
Beloved,
I long only To BE,
US as a Singularity.

Love's Journey

Tarrying in the mine, my Life,
dimly lit by books and talk, faint glints of Love's
sparkled jewels were just enough to keep
the search in earnest.
Through beleaguered eyes this wanderer saw
"US" as another vein, hopeful for more than
trinkets. Despair's clammy arms always a few steps

behind.
Such treacherous passages at times, requiring great negotiating to pass. But always, each new section contained
some new jewel more valuable than all the others combined.
Never had it occurred to mind, that this is Love's journey.
Picking up pieces of the Mother Lode all the Way, one at a time.

Kissed Once

Oh thief, that comes in the night,
kisses my heart
then steals it away in the morning.
What if I were kissed a hundred
or a thousand times...
Is that better, or different?
Do I resist or surrender?
What would make you stay?
Oh thief, that comes in the night,
kisses my heart
then steals it away in the morning.
What if I were kissed a hundred
or a thousand times...

In a Moment's Breath

You have brought the
ancient, to present
the past to Now
the Will to Now
You have brought the
way and the Light to
travel by.
The Song in my Heart...
is Yours.
In Your eyes, I see
my Future is Now;
In You.
Raising me from the
alone valley to
Your mountain side,
My identity capped
by Your Snows.....
My senseless Nothingness,
Your avalanching Stillness;
Shambhala

Changed Scenery

Oh, one of Starry eyes,
seeing through my mask;
you displace the basilisk.
Embracing my steely need,
you unlocked the pouch.
Softness flints my hardness,
sparking out a Dante's Inferno.
Turning to gold from lead,
uncorked a bottled genie's bed.
Spelunking palisades of Openness,
canaries drown within your depths.
Our separation lines suppressed,
a cogent Monet emerges impressed.
Our altering egos Rocked,
now a philosopher's Stone.
Knowing You, bared; Shown,
Realities of Primal Unknown.
As some kept promise of yore,
To return, to that before.
Meeting on how ever many shores;
From Oneness, We parted, nevermore.

What I Want

You may never See me,
or be near me.
This doesn't matter.
My cravings alone,
are enough.
That is because,
You created Them.
Having these Inside,
means You are too.
What more then,
could I ever Want?

Being There

Presence is more than just being there.
'Tis by some design. We are in a position
in space and time to connect.
Orbit closer my moon!
I feel You pulling an ocean from me,
rising tides of immensity.
So strong is Our gravity,
my form is changed from my
middle to my poles.
Eons shall pass before we ever slow
or change... and then, in a collapse
we will fall into each other,
someday... for now I just

watch with longing seas
and smiling mountains.
Continue to share this space,
revolving around each other... and
OUR Sun,
OUR Passion...
As One.

Rant, Ramble, Worship

love lives in Our Home !
it truly does!
not just an expression from the state of observation
Love, truly does live in Our Home!
The fire for the One,
which raged like infinite Suns.
Now, is the inferno of the Beloved's very throne...
Listen! Universe, I declare with all that is sacred,
pure and beautiful...
My heart is full.
My Passion and thirst quenched...
By this One!
Thank you Friend, Father of Lights
for this spark of yourself,
wrapped so tight within my Soul...
You, Beloved.
I am You.

I have tasted Love.
I want only this,
More!
Let me drink...
Let me satisfy the hunger for you.
Let me.
In a thousand turns of the Wheel
I'd trade it all for one moment with you.
This cannot be said.
Words limit it. I rant with the ravings of a Mad Man.
Aye; mad from the intoxicating fever your touch brings.
If I cannot have it again... then only turn your face toward me,
show me your eyes, and that glance would be
Love alive.

I dance.
Glances from you...
My music is ears feeling God's Breath.
This Creation, We created, made by Love's hand.
Some only know like a scholar or student of a mystery,
dreaming of that Reality.
Once touched by the Friend, the finger of Love
penetrates every layer I exist, through all veils,
unfolding my weakness and strength alike.
My will flees as if a flood came upon a house in a valley,
karma stained, damned for so many years,
one lifetime could never have cleansed them.
Here I stand, Your fingerprints everywhere.
Nowhere is safe within myself, anymore.

I will shelter in the only thing left
within the Valley of my Life,
Beloved

Thank you for giving me so much
I just feel so much Love
I don't know if this will ever stop.
It's like looking at the sky, being cut by mountains,
Where is "up", where is "down?"
Yes, a feeling but more than that.
It's a state of Being...

My body, it is quivering for your presence.
When we stand close to each other,
I feel it... something just pulls toward you.
I know infatuation. I know addiction. I know obsession.
This, this goes beyond those!
B-E-Y-O-N-D
Thus Worship

Lakeside

I fell victim again, in this spacious ocean
Looking without and within for a form of You
I rapidly divide myself, creating many new eyes
This burning begins evaporating eyes skyward
Where the seeking continues upon the winds
Pains of separation, brew bursting storm clouds
Rivers collect the tears into ponds and lakes
You decide to visit one, to pick fresh flowers
While hundreds of eyes, with little tails, watch

Harboring

A beacon's brilliant light;
soft sultry cries;
leads a proud, ambitious sailor
to where she lies.
Fathoms deep, the cries sank,
into his Soul;
with hurricane strength force,
her pleasure shoals.
Her waves of surf for him;
the others don't hear;
fear standing down quarterdeck,
courage crow's nest clear.
A callous ship journeys on;
the soft heart disembarks;
one moonbeam, an island's tall
lighthouse parting the dark.

Fish

Let's be fish in the Universe's pond of Love and swim to new depths.
Why poke around on the surface, wishing the scum did not shadow the Sun??
Listen, even the coldest, most barren and frightening deep water contains plumes of life giving minerals and heat.
Venture down far enough and what Father Sun does not provide, Mother Earth will.

Life permeates top to bottom.

The journey up or down is so wonderful with US because the destination is only our current direction, not the requirement for happiness.
No.
Being together, that is the only requirement.
Please continue to swim with me...
Hey! I like this view.
What a pair of fins and tail you have!!!!

Now smile.

By Love

A beautiful impetus
etching time's surface
Breaking wave cresting
onto the golden shores
Star fire dignitary of
all moonlight serenades
Things without a breath
still pulse exaltations
Before the before, after
any after, always present
By Love

Love's Division

In a hundred lifetimes, I will always wait for You!
The moment for eternity, to become real, substantial.
Any ending was premature, for what point was enough?
To have seen those eyes, or have touched Your cheek?
To share a laugh, a cry or twenty nine years together?
Or one night as passionate lovers, or days, one hour?
Do we get to have long conversations or lots of silence?
Are there any choices other than to feel completed by
You?
This You, this connection, is this a never ending journey?

This, says the Angel is the key. To love beyond any
boundary.
The one. To know that behind the mask, is an essence-a
Soul.
It is not the love for the one, it is the two, loving as one.

Blue Knight

My Lady,

I am of the Blue Nights,
The Protectors.
few withstand my sword.

Allow me to lay my Sword
before your seat.

Weaponless I approach.

Here is my shield as well,
For I am already defenseless.

I remove my shin guards, and leg
covers to kneel before you,
Humbled by your beauty.

My helm, I remove,
to meet the stars:
Your eyes.
To smell Lilacs,
your aroma.
To hear angelic chorus,
Your voice,
To taste honeydews,
a kiss of your hand
To touch velvet,
your cheek.

My chest protector,
I remove,
My heart exposed, open to
all you will give,
and all you take.

I am yours

You Know

A blood moon overtakes my soul in silence
You awaken the dark night with sultry eyes
intentional glances eviscerate my solitude
my most deepest aspects now long for You
ripping apart my resolve to understand this
You propel my heart to a joyful wanderlust
whatever the purpose or direction from here
You will always be on my mind, and in my heart

Mark Your Calendar

whenever hands clasp Life, Love touches all
passions roar alive, clawing deep channels
for sweet water baths, where nightingales dip
twenty-seven suns will set before one full moon

You Again

In this missing you, I find the delicacies of indulgence
I am a fraud and imitator of that eastern Lion of lovers
My lonesome husk spills raggedy retinues almost verbatim
Wishing and delirious to hit upon things that elicit you,
not as a record of a past moment, but, of one right now

I scribble on, knowing just thinking of what to put here
will cause me to focus on my feelings and thoughts of You
once started, I become awe struck and struggle to describe
how this comes again, to be inside myself, with only You,
being the only thing ever worth going there for and with

Ready

On the shore of the Emerald sea many walk,
only the company of Birds, attracted to the
spreading seeds of unwavering loneliness
until,
one seagull from the island of many faces
answers the true call, ignoring the seeds
to drink from the eternal heart spring

From the golden center of connecting
ribbons, a scarlet one dangles from
the sky, flirting about
until,
one passionate and fearless reach is
made, by the hand of a Soul now open
and willing to take flight, on faith

Her Dawn, My Birdsong

Bird of Paradise leaps from Her perch,
atop a Douglas Fir, in the Northwest.
Sighting Her flight, I experience Rebirth;
Beating Heart wings, Flocking Hope's Chest

An arrow strung, my quivering Need,
Slivering a Hair, a feathered flight line.
Falling, spinning a vortex's Seed;
Cracked eggshells nested, chirping Sublime

Right now?

Do you want the quiet whisper of I love you,
or the raspy out of breath mumble - I want You, now?
In one accord, voice, intent and focus..... nothing
else matters, only having You... fully.
Surrender. Leave your defense to me...
Nothing else matters, right now- in this. We are
here and we are ready to become One.

Venture the risk and let go... let go...
Lover... Beloved, my desire!

Close your eyes.... feel everything from inside.
Let me take you there, further still... I want to
lose myself with you... Breathe my breath...
Touch my lips with yours and never stop… release your
passion and join me in mine... its burning will grow
even hotter...
Together... our time is now.

Climatic

the air is crisp, clean and cool, spring warm
sateen sheets, enough for a modest beginning
short and deeper breaths, slowly kissed names
exploring bodies, uncovering sensuous secrets
deepening passion, succumbing to an impulsivity
heightening desires, increasing pulses, flexion,
overwhelming senses, submerging pinpoint sensory
point of no return, no control, no holding in
release, pouring out, waves of satisfaction
connection, surreal, ethereal, complete

Rapturously

Beautiful, beautiful lover, flowering
A tulip is crushed within a hand
Releasing the enticing fragrances
His hand caresses her hair, particles
and pieces of flower mix new scents
From sighs to smiles to deep kisses
The embrace tightens, coming closer
His light finger brush paints skin
and shooting stars cross her skies
Never a fleeting urge, his yearning
boils from beneath the mountains, as
A volcano within his Soul, rising
to erupt voluminous flows of passion
That passion hardens and solidifies
into the bedrock of their union
Beautiful, beautiful lover, softly
enfold his offering and become One

Being with You

Together,
To be such a moment as before Now,
would be as One before time...
To be such a place as before Here,
would be as One before space...
Forever.

Close Calls

Beyond my arm's length,
is too far away, to embrace
Beyond a low whispering,
is too far away, to embrace
Beyond this slow dance,
is too far away, to embrace
You.
Stay,
stay the night or morning,
is too far away, to embrace.

Glazed

I can't tell time anymore,
since You came
Days are years, every moment
a surrendering
In any room with You, I want
to borrow sugar
Knowing I have no bowl, You
just cup my hands
Kissing each palm, pressing
them together
The sweetness of Creation
fills my soul
And my lips begin burning
from tasting Heaven

Questioning Love

I once questioned Love,
Love gave no answer.
I was once questioned by Love,
I could give no answer.
Oh, who cares?
I had Love's attention!

my Capture

The greatest edifice is a
tiny mirror reflecting You.
The greatest bridge span is
the longing for You.
My seven wonders are
plundering in the treasure
of You.
Your Midas touch pours
the golden heart mold.
Such a small price to
pay; the ransoming of me,
to the Freedom of You.

Timing My Breaths

Beloved, teach me Your Qi Gong.
taken, taken, gone, gone Beyond
from impermanence, to essence
acquiesce even sentience.
Let me see all Your forms.
Trust my delicate touching
of Your sacred papyrus scrolls.
Whatever is revealed unto me,
slowly whispered, disappears.
My hands will artfully caress the
sculpture You already are; my Star.
Grant the enticement of precisement,
and deliberate movement of moments.
These motions will remind me of
You, when everything happens at once.
Each direction You turn and breathe,
causes my returning six in timed space.
Thus, my breathlessness of Your Oneness.

On the Curb

Look at all the poets brandishing
those instruments of encouragement!
Or the artists and all their posters,
banding the colors of inspiration!
Moreover, the music and its provocative
massaging of hearts to utter softness!
Sometimes there is talk, of this being
Our expression and connection to divinity;
All I know is my epiphany is holding hands
and watching with You, as Life parades by.

Homecoming Day

What will happen Homecoming Day?
Flowers spring into my eyes,
Music plays through my ears,
Sugarcane melts my tongue,
Jasmine incenses my breath,
Sunlight bursts from my heart,
The moment you enter that door!

Stillness

In all the forms that Beauty exists,
Your name is the chime I wish to whisper
To have now, that gentle breeze to echo,
My heart would be strung, spinning freely
Light and floating, my hollow tubular limbs
Move from some cacophony, to a rich fugue
For in the space of the dangling elements
of Being, there is only Breath; one word-
Beloved

Saying Goodbye

Tidings farewell of Love's nest?
Nay!!!
Marching forward toward dawn's glow,
Heart pierced, a blood thickened pool,
Nurtures a new Rose, with fewer thorns.

Surviving

When you are gone,
I can only sleep to dream
of our first dawn
together.
without You entering
the Garden gate;

I can only wait.
Time drips...
drop... by
drop...
My tears,
Life sops 'til
You're Here
Post me,
a lasting bastion,
ramparts of Passion,
crossing to You.
Until that Revival
upon Hearted walls,
standing tall,
I watch for Your arrival.

Preoccupied

I'm tired of the hokey pokey, run 'round!
I need to lose my freaking mind with You!
Let's get rough and raw, like a branding,
and make up all kinds of new things to try!
Someone saying stop, means we got it right!
You know what I want! Things that will make
us think about the next day... and grin.
Better yet, grin and then need to try and
massage out the soreness...
So, how is Saturday night looking for you?

The Forest

Without you here, my chest caves in from pecks given by the crow of separation. Away from you too long and soon they will reach the steaming heart that barely beats now.... the tearing and shredding, I am soon wrought and overcome.... my blood spewing into open chasms of loneliness... it drips down my front, to be refused by any daring enough to partake of its lifelessness..

Mother Earth alone is powerful enough to withstand my condition without a grimace...
Even now my head reels from afar... lands of foreign tongues and unknown delights.... waiting for a Lover that never stays much longer than needed to inflame even worse longing.... only to depart for the horizon... the Sun setting for a month would be less agonizing...

Huge carrion of steel and rubber carry off my prize.... the heart I cannot live without, though not I within my own body.   But the beating of the Beloved's rhythmic breaths into my ear...
Like a giant tree in the stillness of a windless forest... I wait...longing for a shimmer of the nymph's flowing gowns...for her touch that brings the ancient senses to full blossom...like the flowers of a tulip...her touch opens me... and my seeds must come forth..
After the moment of her embrace...the flames of her desire, burn my limbs and trunk into a blackness that becomes my essence... not for a moment do I regret my

existence being changed... the purifying of her gift demands no less... and I am prepared to buy it with my own beauty... to become the sacrificial fire for her altar... The giving and the acceptance... the sublime circle of Love...life for death...surrender for victory...
One fire...
One consummation

I tarry until then... dark forest canopy overhead... inches of decaying mulch upon the forest floor... Rarely a sound this deep into the wilderness... always, my own breathing to accompany my thoughts... thoughts of our meadow... memories of our last union... the wolf searches for the edge of the forest again, and only a wolf that is home here can do such a thing...

a la natural

Love brings a unified Consciousness

He waits in the grove, for her return
after parting from their morning walk
A breeze rustles the elm's senses and
then branches bend touching the grass

The branches are arms that end with
hands and the leaves, but finger tips
The morning dew upon the grass is
the seductive moist lips of nature

He kneels and kisses the ground

Your Choice

Listen again as that stormy word, Love
crashes through the sealed window panes
See too, how Its agent, passion, ignites
some wickless candles into paired lips
Feel Its pressure on the chest, lifting
away breath, and overflowing the heart
Taste the sweetness, as unknown flavors
invade the palate, holding exotic aromas
Awake and walk beyond the transitional
Sleep and dream beyond the confining
Just surrender to It, for It will come
One way, or another

A Jug

Fill this, my cup again, come what may
My bane or a trumpet calling a victory
Conditioned mouths cry for this liberty
Whilst kingdoms may fall hostage to fate
One Lover can change Time's cursing flow
Wondrous courage overtakes a full heart
Changing every experience into an elixir
Seemingly pressed from the Tree of Life
Filled again is my heart, when You come

Soothing

Garish imagery accompanied by a wooing clarinet
memories surrendering the nectar of Your taste
something unfocused and thrilling peeks through
the sheer and floating mist, covering the scene
wishing to squint clarity, blemishes the sounds
of the internal narrative replaying each phrase
word by word and line by line, my smile widens
Despite a great yearning and desire to see You,
the Passion from my Heart was to hear Your voice

Rewind

Yes, in the simple words, everything is clear
Knowing this love, everything became important
As the orchestrated moving melody of Life's
purposes become known, the symmetry of oneness
leaps into awareness.
This insight becomes the guiding light for
anyone willing to look within, since the
light is only visible through an open heart.
Yes, this all sounds cliché, and a bit new age,
but, it is always worth repeating; I love you.

This One Time

With that one look, you dart away
Running again, running nowhere
It must be fearful, this opening
All the projections, pretensions
coverings, and denials - the masks
The pass way to your heart is now bare
Fumble something in the way or stand
weakened and defenseless - naked
The fear is, will this hurt me?
Will I be used, fooled, deceived?
Is this something true, sacred, and
meant to be? Is this the one?
Can this be trusted?
The answer is unequivocally, yes!
Trust to simply be open.
Trust all will work out in the end.
Trust you will survive any result.
Trust everything happens for a reason.
Trust in this moment, right now.
Trust that love will find its way...

Partial Delivery

I have seen you so many times
and looked right through you
You are invisible to the eye
Anything itself contains you

yet, I can't always see that
I only know where you are if
you are hiding away from me
giggling behind the big tree
This great story of lovers
is supposed to be on a beach
with blankets and wine, waves
but, you make the sand angels
Let's lay in the park grass
and watch the star filled sky
not climb trees until scared
The mountain cabin is cozy in
winter with the fire blazing,
not what animals come at night
I can show you all the things
that make up a romantic love
it has all been written down
Sure there is something that
is erotic, sensual, focused
on the connection, and just
a bit teasing, not idealized,
brisk, playful, stirring and
spiritually attuned to today
There may be no eroticism now
but, we have the rest, here

Two into One

She was the faceless
silhouette in a dreamscape
jewel of the Nile
A blooming desert
casting her shadow awash
curving bronze statue
Flying chariot
deliver secret messages
whispers of silk sheets

Yesterday a man
fading memories of night
the queen crowns the king
Reigning together
resolved to becoming one
creating a Sphinx

Flights of

Being with You I feel tiny
not knee high, size of a bee
You say, then ride the world
from the back of a hummingbird
we have little oak slippers,
gripping a leaf stem rope to
cope and not fall off, up quick
the slick Green feathers, we

hang on tight, flying up the
tree, You duck, I get hit by
a leaf, turn left, turn right
following a crooked flight
branches split ahead, we flick
right, higher and higher we
hit the top, and see the Sun,
now back down, round and round
the trunk, whirling side to side
we stop midway at a hollow,
a starling flies by, staring
we sit for a bit, holding hands
and a small little kiss, a
peck really, then we knock
our feet against the bark
hollow sounding, a woodpecker
comes calling, we hop on its
back, to get to the ground,
such joy and fun, with the One
I feel like the swallows do
returning to Capistrano

Redemption

Love redeems only two things;
Surrender and Gratitude

Consigned

something of wisdom
fell from the sky
longing against tears
the shameless rush in
with a Copernican view
the heavens tell us
the fates that awaited
these cosmic swirls and
movements, are ciphers
only a few understand

then in any mind that
looks at the moon, or
a star, sees patterns,
the beauty, uniqueness
and with that, decides
to witness, to confess
there is only mystery
that mind realizes that
the astrologers and the
astronomers are the same

Absent thee

Come Horatio, from behind the enclave
give the soliloquy, the lullaby for Aphrodite,
bring down the curtain, open the partition,
cursed eyes of fate, crying destiny's attrition,
crimson and bombastic, draping anguished tears,
eroding consoles, footing slipperiness,
paving cobblestone throughway to perdition
Go Horatio, back behind the enclave

Take Heart

Destiny arrived heartbroken and shattered,
Wearing the remnants of forgotten claims
Hope appearing powerless with ineptitude,
To cross paths with their chance encounter

Little Soul without your twin's imprint,
Be fearless, return to sleep and dream
The Friend promises a gentle awakening,
Where every love story knows how to end